2014

Christian Development
Organization

Shakeel Nouman

[DAIRY GOAT PRODUCTION]

Shakeel Nouman,
M.Phil (Statistics), Government College University, Lahore.
Phone # +923219898767, E-mail.sn_gcu@live.com.

Farmers Handbook

DAIRY GOAT PRODUCTION

Mr. Shakeel Nouman

M.Phil (Statistics), Government College University Lahore

Dr. Yasir Abrar

M.Phil (Dairy Technology), University of Veterinary & Animal Sciences

FORWARD

This farmers booklet on rearing dairy goats was written and prepared by FARM Researcher Mr. Shakeel Nouman. The booklet has been prepared using simple language that farmers can understand. Hence the efforts are to avoid technical language. Writers share their Farm experiences with farmers.

The growing demand for dairy goats within and outside Pakistan has prompted us to prepare this booklet for farmers who may acquire goats from the FARM Pakistan project in Okara and need skills for rearing/keeping the goats.

Thorough and detailed information for those who may need can be obtained from a book by FARM Pakistan, Dr. Mumtaz Hussain Improving Goat Production in the Tropics.

Writer's of the booklet are Mr. Shakeel Nouman, Dr. Yasir Abrar of Livestock Production Research Institute Bahadurnagar(Okara).

This booklet was produced in collaboration with Veterinary Doctors.

Table of Content

13.	• From Toggenburg valley • Brown in colour • White line on the face, legs and tail • Male weigh between 70-IIOkgs while female weigh 60-70kg live body weight • Produces up to 5 litres of milk per day • Has a little bit higher butter-fat content	
14.	**3. Anglo-Nubian** A cross breed of Nubian (sudan) and English goats.	
15.	• White and dropping ears • Male weighs between 70-110 kgs live body weight • Females weigh 60-70 kgs live body weight • Its milk has a high butter-fat content • Produces up to 5 litres milk per day • Its milk is good for making cheese due to high butter fat content • Has long dropping ears	
16.	**4. German Alpine/British Alpines**	
17.	• Black in colour • Produces up to 3 litres per day • Shorter than Toggenburg	
18.	**5. Obernhesili**	
19.	• Brownish in colour • Gives up to 3 litres per day	
20.	**6. Galla** (also referred to as Boran or Somali goat) **CONCLUSION**	
21.	• Goats are well adapted to many environments • There are many breeds of dairy goats available for use • The genetic diversity of goats should be better understood and • respected • Goats can overgraze and damage the environment if not looked • after properly • Goats are a very good source of income and food if well managed	

1.WHY KEEP DAIRY GOATS?

1.1. Goat's milk is good! Goat's meat is tasty!

- Goats Milk is easy to drink and is a richer food because it has more calcium, phosphorous and chlorine than cow's milk.

- Milk is used at home so that the families get the best milk - if there is a cow many farmers will sell the cows milk for cash and make sure the family gets the goat milk to drink!

- Tasty Meat! Goat's meat is very tasty and it is juicy and eaten often by many people

- More and more people are learning about how good goat's milk, cheese and yoghurt are so there is a growing market

- Goat's milk is better for the family as it has a "High Nutritional Content." This means it is a very high quality food and very good for young and old.Some people cannot drink cow's milk. They have an "allergy" to it. This is why some children are reared on goat's milk when cow's milk and all else has failed. Nobody is allergic to goat's milk!

1.2. Goat - Cow - Human milk contents

	GOAT	COW	HUMAN
Protein %	3.0 *	3.0	1.1
Fat %	3.8	3.6	4.0
Calories/100ml	70 *	69	68
Vitamin A (i.u./gram fat	39 *	21	32
Vitamin B (UG/100 ml)	68 *	45	17
Riboflavin (ug/100 ml)	210 *	159	26
Vitamin C (mg ascorbic acid/100 ml) 2	2*	2	3
Vitamin D (i.u. /gram fat)	0.7 *	0.7	0.3
Calcium	0.19 *	0.18	0.04
Ron	0.07 *	0.06	0.2
Phosphorus	0.27 *	0.23	0.06
Cholesterol (mg/100/ml)	*Low is	15	20

*Shows the best nutrition

1.3. Make more money!

- Get cash from selling milk

- Get a higher price for goat milk
- Get kids every year (twice per year) and sell them easily when ready
- Kids can be twins/triplets
- With small farm sizes it is a better way to earn money and feed the family
- In the space and using the same feed you need to keep a cow you can keep 6 goats!
- Do not need big areas to graze like cattle
- Farmers can pay school fees using income from sale of milk/manure
- Products fast and easy to sell
- Goats sell easily for meat
- Many people prefer goat cheese
- Start getting benefits quickly
- Uses small doses of drugs - cheap. Easy to maintain
- Good for people who do not have a lot of money to start with

**Goats make very good manure. Droppings are used to improve crop yields

1.4. Goats are good for the shamba
- Less feed is needed to keep a goat than a cow
- Goats will eat many different plants - so easier to keep fed through the year
- Droppings are used as manure for organic farming

- Goats good at keeping bush under control -stops too much shrub growth
- Will live even where there is a drought. Does not need a lot of water and can go for quite a long time without water in very dry times

1.5. Important for Social events
- Goats are used traditionally as payment of dowry
- Goats are often eaten during land cases, parties, clan meetings etc.

- Goats are important in some rituals, they are used during circumcision ceremonies for example
- Goat horn and bone are used in the traditional craft industry

1.6. Do not need to work so hard!

- Goats require less labour and time per head compared to cattle

2. HOUSING THE GOAT

2.1.A good goat house will make keeping goats easier.

- Rain proof
- Damp proof
- Well ventilated
- Free from direct wind
- Free from sharp objects t

- might cut the goat
- Pest and wild animal
- proof
- Slats on floor for free fall of droppings
- With an area of at least 2 meters per animal

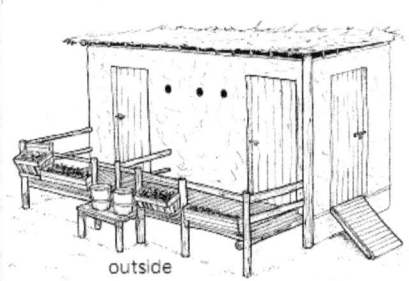

outside

If you build a goat house like the one shown then you will:
- Animals do not get sick very often
- You can make sure that only the animals you want to breed do so
- Make it very easy to feed
- Stop wasting feed
- Save the goats wasting energy and increase the amount of milk you get
- Keep goat's feet dry and clean all the time

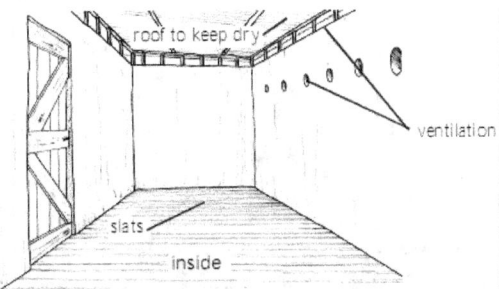

A GOOD HOUSE MEANS HEALTHY GOATS

2.2.Types of Houses
When you start you may not have a lot of money to make a house.
But as it is very important to have a house you can make the first one with local materials.

Mud houses

This is the cheapest house to build because it uses local materials:

- Posts
- Mud
- Rafters for floor
- Nails
- Grass for thatch roof
- When placing mud,make holes in the wall slanting down so that,the air does not land directly on the goats

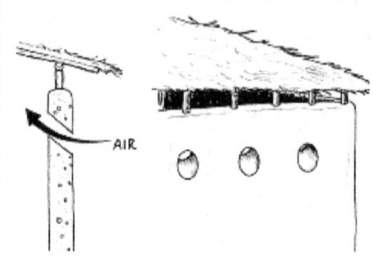

"Off cuts" houses

This house costs a little more but it will last longer Materials:

- Posts
- Off-cut planks
- Nails
- Iron sheets or gras for thatching
- Wood - rafters or planks for the floor

2.3.The house

There are two main areas of the house, the sleeping area and feeding area.

Sleeping area

- Wall right around - with a door
- It must be roofed
- Lots of air allowed in (well ventilated)

Feeding area

- Open not roofed, goats need some   sun
- Fence right around with a door/gate
- Feed trough/water area Place for hanging fodder [feed Racks]
- Floor with slats to let manure fall through - keeps feet and animals clean and dry
- Place to hang mineral block (placed where it cannot be rained on)

2.4.The house parts

Floor

- House should be raised 1.5 feet (or just below knee height) from the ground.
- A slatted wooden floor is very important.This has small gaps - about half an inch wide (or the width of a side of a match box) between the planks or rafters
- Use of local materials means you can use off cut planks,etc.
- The floor racks made of rafters should be put where the goats feed and sleep, this stops foot rot when it is wet, keeps clean and dry

Kid Pen

- Toggenburgs often give birth to twin kids so don't

Hay Barn/Store;

- To store fodder, for use during the dry season, build a store adjacent to the goat house that is roofed to avoid hay being rained on

Mineral Trough

- Should be made where the goats sleep
- A one [1] foot square box is ideal for the purpose.A halved long ways plastic con- tainer nailed to a board,at least 1 foot wide can be useful
- Or just as good - hang the salt so the goat has to reach for it

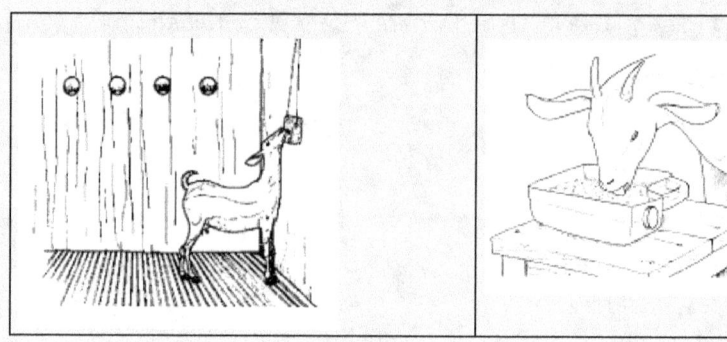

PLAN FOR GOAT HOUSE
Plan for 4 Does. 1 Buck.6 Kids

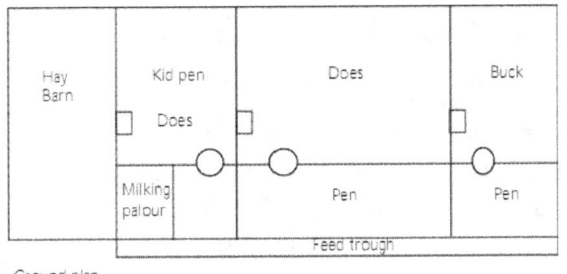

Ground plan

3. FEEDING OF THE DAIRY GOAT

3.1. How does a goat like to eat?
A goat does not like to graze on the ground like a sheep, buffalo or cow

Goats like feeding at knee height up to head height so they like to feed above the ground often standing on their hind legs and resting their fore legs up on the bush or goat house wall.

Goats need to be able to drink fresh water at all times

Advantages of stall feeding

- Does not need a large amount of land and no grazing pastures
- Can use many farm products, banana leaves, maize, maize thinnings,bean husks,etc.
- Saves time and labour, do not have to take goats out of the shamba for grazing or spend time looking for them
- Less death amongst the kids and all goats because they can be easily looked after throughout the day
- Easier to plan and manage breeding
- Keeps goats from eating crops and damaging the shamba
- Makes collecting manure very easy
- Helps in controlling diseases

What do they eat?

- They eat a lot of different plants/feeds. But they know what they want to eat
- They prefer some plants/feeds to others
- They even prefer different parts of the plant so they will eat leaves and

flowers and not pods or stems, within the same plant

- They get bored when fed the same feed everyday
- They can be wasteful. Only eating some of the plant. For example given un-chopped feeds like napier grass they pull it out of the ground, eat the leaves only and do not eat the stem
- Are clean feeders, and will not eat dairy feeds which are not fresh nor dirty feed e.g.napier with mud splash from rain
- Do not like sticky, mouldy, wet dusty feeds

3.2.The best way to feed goats

- Feed only clean, fresh and dry fodder
- Always have fresh water for goats to drink at
- Clean the feeding trough and water bucket every day
- Give lots of different feeds such as grasses and legumes, tree leaves and fresh kitchen remains
- Give chopped mixed feeds to make sure the goats eat everything and does not waste feed
- Feed goats at least 3 times a day and at the same time every day
- Put some feed in the feed trough or rack or hang up some feed to be eaten overnight
- If you use molasses to make feed taste better do not use too much it will make feed sticky
- Dusty feeds and concentrates should be wetted a little.
- Provide fresh and clean water daily. There should always be water in the bucket
- Provide a Mineral Lick [block] always to all goats.
- Do not feed too much leguminous feed such as desmodium
- Mix feeds with grass,hay, straw or napier to balance
- Only 1/3 of the days feed can be leucenea, Do not feed too much leucenea,it can poison the goats

Chop Napier so whole plant is eaten

3.3. Feeding different goats

Remember all goats must have fresh water whenever they need it

Feeding sick goats
- Feed goats well when ill. Good feeding will give strength
- Small, weak, young and sick goats should be fed separately
- Follow the best way to feed goats carefully and handle gently

Feeding mature goats
- Should be fed on whatever feed there is - enough to keep well and keep the animals weight

Feeding the buck
- Feeding should be enough to keep its weight steady but not too fat
- A fat buck will not be active and its weight
- Give more feed two months before the buck has to
- serve the does this will improve the bucks sperm and make it more active
- When a buck is being used a lot to serve does,
- it should be separated from other goats for
- about 2-3 hours per day. This will allow it
- time to eat as well as serve the does
- Lots of fresh and clean water needed all the time
- Must be able to lick the mineral lick at any time

Feeding does
- Concentrates should be fed to Does just before the does are served by the buck
- Increase feed gradually for 2 months up until the doe gives birth
- Continue feeding concentrate while she is giving milk

The doe needs careful feeding in order to:
- Keep its normal weight up,
- Be fertile when served so as to get twins (Flushing)

- Carry the kid while it is pregnant
- Give milk to its kids
- Give extra milk for farmers use

Feeding the breeding and lactating doe

- One month before mating the doe should be fed and watered very well so as she is in the best of health.
- If she is very well she is more likely to have twins or even triplets
- Mineral licks hasten comming on heat
- Give lots of water at all times

Feeding during pregnancy

First 3 months of pregnancy

- The goats needs to be fed as normal and to be sure that she is healthy

The last two months of pregnancy

- The goat must be fed well with high quality feed
- The "foetus" or kid inside does nearly all it's growing in this period
- There may be twins or triplets and they will need lots of good feed to grow

During first 2 months after Kids birth and giving milk

- The goat must be fed so it can give lots of good milk and keep its own weight up
- Can be supplemented with at least 200 gm/day of dairy meal.
- Reduced to 100gm/day during the 3rd month

Feeding kids

Feeding the newborn up til 3 months

- Newborn kids should suck colostrum within 24 h and then should be with the doe and allowed as m as they need
- At one week, kids should be provided with small quantities of good clean feed e.g. sweet potato vin tree legumes leaves or natural tree leaves
- Kids should continue with milk for the first three weeks, and thereafter be allowed milk with fresh mixed fodder up to 3-4 months.

young stock

- Should be fed on fresh, highly nutritious mixed fodder
- Give lots of water at all times
- Provide lots of water
- Mineral blocks must be given at this stage

3.4.What kind of feed should the goat be given?

The dairy goat gives as much milk as it is given the right food!! There are many feeds the goat likes. Here are some good feeds that can be used.

Sweet potato vines

- This is a very good feed that goats like very much
- It is a good crop to plant because it gives tubers for the family to eat and the leaves can be fed to the goats
- It can be planted beside river beds,steep parts of the shamba and road-side edges
- Useful in feeding kids whose mothers die early in thier life.

Napier

- Plant napier along river beds,along soil terraces, road reserves etc.
- Where a farmer has a big shamba then plant as one crop near the home to save time and work when taking to the goats
- Good napier needs manure and top dressing with a fertilizer and needs weeding
- Where new fields are being planted mixed cropping with desmodium improves the quality of the fodder
- If you plant Napier around your maize it stops Maize stalk borer!

- Cut Napier often so it is easy for the goats to eat and digest

Fodder trees and legumes

- These have lots of protein and you need only feed a little at a time
- These are for example: leuceana, calliandra,sesbania and desmodium
- The trees and legumes,should be planted along the fences and terraces

Leuceana is good in fences

- Good legumes are potato vines,
- They do not need a lot of work once they are growing
- Desmodium when available should be inter-cropped with Napier
- Calliandra does better in high altitudes (tea zones) than leuceana
- Do not forget that many weeds also make good fodder

Maize

While maize is grown for farmer's food, there is a lot of fodder which can be used for feeding the goat which will not stop the farmer getting a good maize yield

- Thinning - all the extra maize seedlings that grow from the same seed
- hole should be thinned and dried a little before feeding to the goats.
- Remove extra leaves - this should start with the leaves below the cobs as soon as the cob can be seen.

Cutting the tops - this should start after the grains have hardened.

- Stovers - these should have sweeteners (molasses) added or sprinkle common salt after chopping.
- Broken grains - these are very nutritious especially after a heavy harvest but should be fed carefully to avoid grain overload

4. KIDDING

This is the birth of young goats - Kids
It takes 5 months for a goat to give birth after it has been served, by a male

4.1. Preparation for kidding

There are three very important rules for kidding.

Rule 1: Ensure the kidding doe is put in a dry clean and quiet place at the time of kidding.

Rule 2: The kidding place should be under a shelter (in the house) or shade.This is to protect the kid from too much sun

Rule 3: The Doe must have water as soon as she has given birth so she can make sure she has enough to balance the loss of water from giving birth and to have enough milk to feed the new born.

Kidding should be done where you can see what is happening easily and often.

4.2. Signs of kidding
- Enlarged vulva
- Restlessness of the doe
- Doe seeks a quiet place away from other goats
- Udder is enlarged, full and firm
- Muscles either side of tail will become sunken and on either side of tail a hollow appears
- Often stand or lie down and stretch her neck pointing her head skyward.
- Will have a clear discharge from the vulva

4.3. Kidding process
- Keep the kid in a cool dry place away from too much heat and draught
- Disinfect the navel immediately using a disinfectant e.g. dettol or tincure of iodine
- Ensure kid suckles colostrum
- within 20-30 minutes after birth
- Stimulate mother-kid bond by encouraging mother to lick the kid
- In case of breathing problems,help by tickling the tongue, and removing
- all mucus from the nostrils

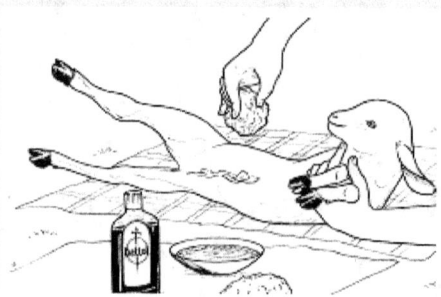

Helping the doe during kidding
Try and make sure everything is as clean as possible
- Normally goats do not have problems giving birth or kidding but sometimes a kid may get stuck during the process of birth
- If you need to help then be sure that before doing so that you wash hands with dettol, make sure nails are cut and remove any jewelry - like rings

- If you can get proper plastic gloves use these to protect yourself and the goat from infections
- When helping kids to be delivered be gentle and make sure you understand the problem before exerting any force
- Be careful when pulling the kids legs that the head is forward and down
- Be careful that you are dealing with one kid at a time and not holding one foot from two kids

Care of orphans
- Foster orphans to docile does or bottle feed with other goats milk or milk replacers.
- May use sweet potatoe vines to feed orphans.

5. HUSBANDRYTECHNIQUES
Once the kid is born there are a number of things to be done

5.1. Disbudding
- This is removal of very young horns that have not grown
- Usually done first to second week of age
- Should be performed by a vet using a hot iron under general anaesthesia using a drug called SAFFAN

5.2. Castration
- Male goats that will not be bred should be castrated early in life (in the first 2 months) and kept for meat
- Can be done by use of rubber rings, burdizzo castrator, or open methods

Rubber rings A2
- Using an applicator insert the Rubber to the testis as shown, make sure it is as high as possible

- Make sure the testis are in the scrotum, below the ring and release carefully
- This can be done on farm after a little practice

Rubber Ring   Application of rubber Ring

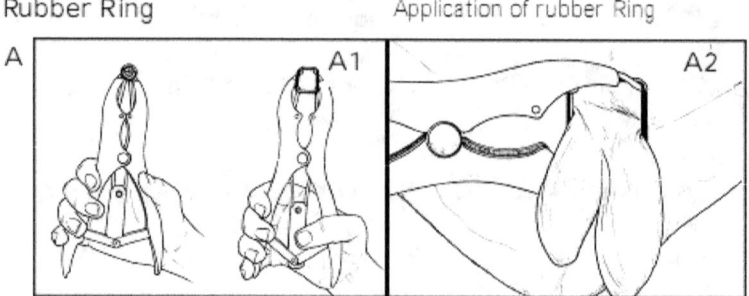

Burdizzo B2

- Hold the spermatic cord with your fingers right at the top, one testicle at a time
- Clamp the Burdizzo on one cord and press the levers to snap it. Repeat for the other testicle

Burdizzo

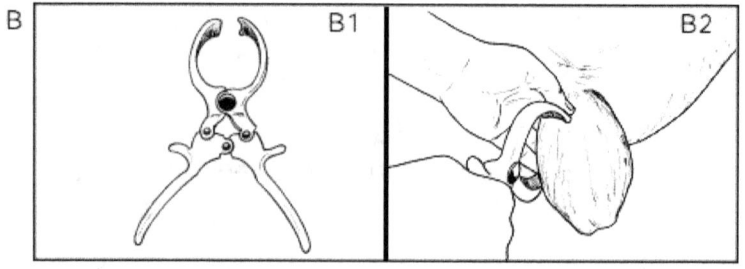

Bur diz zo

Open methods

- It's complete remove of testis by an operation
- This is an operation that you can request your vet to perform for you in cases of trouble

5.3. Identification

Farmers need to be able to identify their animals so they can keep records and easily know the age, breeding and usefulness of each animal

Done through

- Tattooing
- Ear tags
- Paint or ink

- Branding
- Other marks or names
- Extension staff can demonstrate this to farmers interested

5.4. Other managerial practices

Weaning - removing kids from it's mother
- Usually done at 2-3 months of age
- Let kids try hay and grains early in life to strengthen their stomachs
- When you start to wean young goats they will begin to feed on solid
- food. So they will begin to pick up diseases such as Coccidiosis.
- When kids start eating fodder they will suffer high worm infection so they need to be dewormed after exposure
- When given concentrates kids are likely to suffer Enterotoxiemia so you will need to vaccinate against these diseases
- Don't stop feeding milk suddenly but this should be gradual to avoid indigestion or bloat

Hoof trimming
- Do not let hooves grow longer than shown below, cut and trim carefully

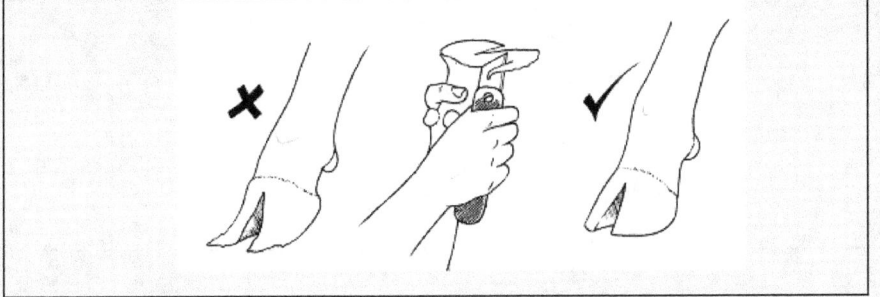

6. MILKING

6.1. Keeping milk clean

The most important thing to do is keep yourself, your hands and buckets, clean. Also carefully clean the doe's udder.

Milking shed

The milking shed should be cleaned after each milking and disinfected

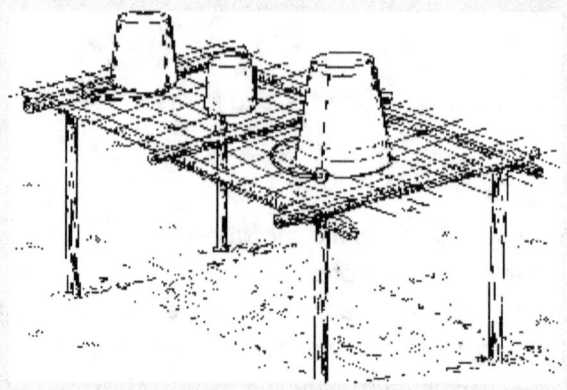

Human infectious diseases
- People who are ill should not milk.

Washing hands
- Before starting milking, the milker should wash his hands, arms with soap and hot water, or disinfectant Keep finger nails cut and clean

Wash Udder
- Before milking the udder should be washed with clean water which has disinfectant added to it.
- Use two cloths alternatively for washing the udders. Leave one in the disinfectant whilst the other is in use.

Cut out bacteria
- The first drop of milk from each teat should be thrown away as it has a very high bacterial count.

6.2. Hand milking

- Good milking is done by the squeeze method.
- Avoid the pulling technique as it hurts the udder and the teat and udder will get a mastitis infection.

The squeeze method of milking
- Take hold and squeeze the base of the teat with the thumb and forefinger to trap the milk in the teat.
- Close the other three fingers squeeze downwards in turn.
- The milk in the teats is squeezed downwards and not pulled.
- Squeezing slowly downward makes the milk come out. Repeat this in a rhythm and quickly-using the full hand to avoid finger and thumb striping.
- This should take about 7 minutes. So be quick so that you get as much milk as possible

Other important dairy goat precautions during milking;
- Always house/pen the doe and the serving buck in different pens to prevent smell in the milk
- Make the milking parlour far from the buck pen
- Wind direction should be from milking palour to the buck pen and not vice versa
- Always be calm, friendly to the doe and milk at the same time every day
- Maintain similar milking position (Back position or side position)
- The nails on the hand of the milker should be short
- Measure and record your milk immediately
- Wash milk equipment with hot water rinse and dry on a rack immediately after milking
- Avoid giving feeds with strong smells just before milking and during
- milking e.g.silage, pineapple, waste etc to avoid tainting the milk
- The hair on the flanks and around the udder should be trimmed regularly and the goat brushed occasionally
- Use of sprays/oils/soaps with smell by milker will taint the milk

After milking tips
- Irregular milking can lead to low yields and increased chance of mastitis.
- The kid should be allowed to suck the milked teat after milking for proper emptying of teat canal
- After milking use a teat dip containing a suitable antiseptic e.g.Tincture of iodine

- If possible same person should milk always

Mastitis

- Goats with mastitis should be milked last to prevent the spread of the infection to other goats
- Mastitis can reduce yields by at least 10%.
- Milk from sick goats, especially goats with mastitis should not be sold but be discarded
- Isolate the goat with mastitis
- Sick animals must be treated

Dry off a doe

If a doe has been served and is pregnant - special care is required during the 4th and 5th month as the embryo's gains weight rapidly.

- The does should be housed alone to avoid disturbance by the other goats
- The doe is dried gradually i.e milking is done normally but the amount milked at every subsequent milking is reduced gradually until finally one stops
- This prevents development of milk clots

7. BREEDING

7.1 What type of goats are available

- Farmers keep local goats. They have been keeping these goats for many years. These goats however do not produce enough milk for their kids and extra for human consumption.
- Goats can be classified as dairy or meat type.
- The local goats are mainly meat types.
- The local goats can survive and thrive in the hot climate, low quality forages and fodder and to some extent resistant to common diseases.
- This makes them produce very little milk.
- The dairy types include the following Toggenburg, Saanen, Alpine, Anglo-Nubian.
- Dairy type goats produce a lot of milk but do not adapt very well.
- These dairy goats are normally mated to local goats to get a goat that is "A better milk producer than the local goats but which are easier to raise than the pure dairy types. The mating of two different type breeds of animals is called crossbreeding.

7.2.What can be done to improve the productivity of the

local goats?

- Feed them properly with different grasses and shrub browses Keep them in a properly built goat house
- Give them good husbandry, treatment
- Cross breed them with improved goat breeds like Toggenburg
- Keep records to help you in knowing and managing your goats

7.3.Why should farmers keep dairy goats

- Farms are becoming smaller as each new generation inherits land - Goats can be kept on small pieces of land
- Goats can be fed on farm by products

7.4.Why breed your goats

- Breeding helps the farmer to have more animals
- With good breeding you get more and better animals
- Good breeding means a farmer has to know his animals and taking good care of them
- A farmer can know his / her animals by keeping records on his / her animals and the events taking place.
- Animals of different ages need different attent ion
- Does, bucks and kids should all be given good care appropriately

7.5.Taking good care of dairy goats

- Well fed and health parents, good offspring
- Both does and buck must be well fed and cared for before becoming parents
- Keep does and bucks apart
- Allow mating to occur at the right time
- Keep a record of dates
- A doeling come into heat at 4 to 5 months of age therefore must be raised apart from bucks from 4 months
- You should mate your doe when it is over 1 year old
- To get good results a farmer must control his goats
- First mating will depend on age and condition of the goat
- Mating before one year should only be allowed provided before and during   pregnancy
- It is recommended that a doe should be bred when she each 75% to 80% of its mature weight
- For milking does they should be bred after the third month of kidding

7.6.When should you breed your does?

A goat can only be bred when she is ready. This condition is referred to as "the goat is on heat"

What are heat signs
- The goats becomes restless and mount each other - Cries loudly and sometimes bleating
- The vulva may became swollen
- The goat wags the tail
- Frequent urination
- Lasts 2 - 3 days

When to mate
- A doe should be mated 12 to 24 hrs after you have seen her on heat
- Heat signs in the afternoon,the goat should be mated the next morning - Heat signs in the morning should be mated in the evening

7.7. Avoid mating goats that are related.

When goats that are related are mated this is called inbreeding.
- Inbreeding should be avoided in animal production
- Inbreeding results in weak offspring,decreased productivity e.g milk and even death
- Bucks should therefore be rotated or moved from their stations after one and half years
- Keeping good records will help a farmer to know which animals are related and which ones are not.

7.8. Keeping Records

Why keep records
- Helps you to know your goats
- Recording increases animal values and therefore sales income - Recording promotes increased milk yields
- Recording promotes improved genetic merit
- Helps you to manage your animals well

Which records to keep
A farmer should keep simple records of
- Birth dates
- Birth weights
- Sire and dam

- Milk records
- Treatment records
- Service dates

Good record on service date will help you calculate the expected date of birth after breeding. You can know the expected date by counting 5 months from the date of service and take off three days

7.9. How can you know your goat is pregnant after mating?

- 3 weeks later doe not on heat
- 8 weeks later the vulva shows an enlargement
- 12 weeks later the abdomen enlarges noticeably

Abortions in goats are not common, but can be avoided by protecting the doe against difficult situations keeping the does well fed and disease free. A pregnant doe should be dried up three months into its pregnancy

7.10. Signs of approaching birth
- A few days before there will be discharge for the vulva
- On the day of kidding,the doe bleats, paws the bedding and becomes restless
- With proper feeding and management, goats normally give multiple births

8. GOAT HEALTH

8.1.Sick goat: How to identify
- Sick goat stands apart from the others in a group. (Animals about to give birth also behave like this)
- They are restless
- They do not lie down and rest even when others in their group do so unless it gets very ill
- They hold their head down
- They have dull eyes and show little interest in their surroundings
- Often have rough coat and look weak and tired
- Do not like to feed

8.2. Kids
The death of kids before they are weaned is perhaps the single biggest cause of loss experienced by goat farmers.

Diseases to watch out for in kids some of the disease could also affect Adult goats

Symptoms	Treatment	Prevention	Notes
a.Coccidiosis			
• Sudden onset of Diarrhoea • Foul smelling faeces containing mucus and blood. • Anus smeared with blood stained faeces • Sudden death may occur • Severe straining • Eat less • Common in housed goats.	• The disease dies out on its own, so to save deaths you must treat at first signs • Give sulphur antibiotics or a drug called coccid	• Reduce stock rate • Clean and make sure pens are well drained and dry • Minimise fouling of feed and • water with faeces, hair, fleece etc. • Use of coocidiostats in feeds to • keep egg level low but allow • goats to become immune	
b. Colibacillosis			
• Fever at the beginning and later, fever drops down • Mouth dry and cold • Diarrhoea (yellowish to whitish) • Depression and weakness • Goat found lying down • Survivors of the infection may show nervous signs and problems with joints	• Give plenty of clean water (oral fluids) • Give antibiotic preparation on vets advice • Isolate affected goats • Treat new cases immediately •	• Give colostrum at birth • House new born kids separately • Disinfect the navel with iodine • solution at birth • Avoid contamination of feeds and utensils by keeping clean • Avoid overcrowding • Regular feeding should be kept	
c. Colostrum deprivation			
• Dry mouth • Fever • Severe weakness • Most die.	• Use oral antibiotics on vets advice	• Cleanliness of the pen • Quarantine of kidding pen if diseases occurs with kids • Clamp and disinfect the navelGive 10% of birth weight of colostrum in the first 24hours • Avoid moving late-	

		pregnant does to new, distantlocations to avoid exposing their off springs to infections of which they have not met before • Supervise birth to make sure births and animals do not get cold or too high temperatures.
d. Enterotoxemia		
• Sudden depression and deaths of kids • Unable to eat • Fluid,brown feaces,some with blood or green pasty diarrhoea • Fever • Death within 2-4 days • Drunken appearance • Lies on side when close to death, paddling legs	• Use oral antibiotics on vets advice	• Reduce feed intake • Vaccination with clostridial vaccines 3 to 4 weeks of age and then boost at 6 to 7 weeks and finally at 6 months • Give concentrates gradually to kids
e. Internal Parasites		
• Sudden death • May have swelling under chin • Anaemia, and weakness. • Post Mortem by a vet will reveal • parasites in intestines,esp. • haemon chus contortus • in stomach • Poor exercise tolerance • Severe weight loss • Break in hair/falling off of hair	• Use dewormers • All dewormers could be grouped into three - yellow - white - colourless • Always start by using them in the following order for each animal you deworm • 1st and 2nd deworming - use yellow • 3rd and 4th deworming - use white	• Avoid contaminated feeds • Deworm just before the rains and after • Good housing prevents contamination of

	• 4th and 5th deworming - use colourless • No physical signs of disease. • Can occur if many kids and adults • are kept together, especially in cold climates.	feeds with feaces.	
f. Suffocation			
• No physical signs of disease. • Can occur if many kids and adults are kept together, especially in cold climates	• First aid if found not dead	• Don't overstock the kid pens	
8.3. MALNUTRITION			
• Weakness,no stomach fill • Dramatic fall in milk production • Staggery gait and recumbence • when deprivation is severe • Weight loss • Mental depression	• In cases of complete deprivation • give small amounts of highly • digestible carbohydrates and • protein feeds through the mouth. • Avoid fats	• Feeds should be balanced diets- • proteins, carbohydrates etc • Feed 3 times a day with water • and mineral block always easy to get	
8.4. ADULT GOATS			
• Kids as well could also get these diseases below			
Mastitis			

This is an infection of the udder. • Fever, toxaemia • Lameness on affected side • Swelling, gangrene of udder, belly wall • The udder will become hot and painful. • Milk is watery and contains clots of bloods	Milk twice a day • Apply antibiotics via the teat as instructed by the vet • In severe cases of infection,an injection of antibiotics may be necessary. • After weaning check the udders of esp. high yielding goats for mastitis. • Frequent milking and massaging of the affected udder NB. Precaution should be taken because misuse of drugs could lead to resistance.Ask for vet's advice	• Could result from failure to milk completely, injuries as a result of pulling teats during milking there-fore milking completely and use of squeeze method instead of pulling will prevent,use tinture of iodine to dip teats.After milking clean the milking area thoroughly after milking • Milk the affected quarter last • Good clean hands, equipment and teats at all times • Provide clean bedding area • Wash hands clean before milking.	
a.Pneumonia			
• Coughing, • Breathing with difficults • Running nose • Fever • Often breath through the mouth as when severe • seem to fight to get	•	•	•

air and may stretch their necks out,trying to get air. N B:Even healthy animals cough occasionally especially if they eat dry dusty foods.			
b.(Pneumonia) Pasteurellosis			
• Goats usually become sick 7-10 • days after they get infected. • Disease spreads fast in a group. • Mostly results from stress, which • could be due to management, cli- • mate or feeding of the goats. ## Prevention • Avoid any stress related conditions in the goats • House in a well ventilated house • Mix fodder as much as possible Nb:The disease is also called ship-ping fever because you stress animals when transported and they get the disease	• Goats stop eating and look tired • and weak.They have a high fever. • They often cough a lot and have • distressed breathing that becomes • worse. • Some animals collapse and die in a few hours. • Other animals are sick from several days. • They lose weight and become thin and weak. Sometimes they have a swollen abdomen. • They grind their teeth. • Their breathing is often rapid but weak.	• Use antibiotic injections early enough • Remove the cause of stress	

	• They usually have diarrhoea. • They die after 5-6 days if they are not treated.		
Worms			
• Goats get worms from fodder which hold many worm eggs or larvae. • Goats can suffer very severe disease. Adult goats suffer as much as young ones. • Usually can be source of stress in goats. • Lungworms will cause the goat to cough and no fever. • Worms in goats can cause death • Eggs may be observed in feaces. • Do not grow well even with good food. • Rough coat. • May have a swelling under the jaw and may • also have swelling under the abdomen. • May have diahhroea	• Use dewormers • All dewormers could be grouped into three – yellow - white - colourless • Always start by using them in the following order for each animal you deworm • 1st and 2nd deworming - use yellow • 3rd and 4th deworming - use white • 4th and 5th deworming - use colourless	• Avoid contaminated feeds • Deworm before the • rains and just after • Good housing that • prevents • contamination of • feeds with feaces. 	
Tick borne diseases In areas infected with ticks, the following diseases are likely to occur: *1. Nairobi sheep*	• No treatment • Vaccine are effective but seek vet's advice	• Transmitted by ticks • Spray or dip the goats	

diseases Goats get it from infected ticks,they do not get it from direct contact with other animals. Only animals that have had the infection become sick. Animals that move for the first time to areas with infected ticks get severe diseases.Sometimes animals bring infected ticks to areas where the disease has not happened. Disease is caused by a virus. • A grey/white discharge comes from the nose and eye. • Goats have diahhroea. • Feaces are often green and watery with blood and mucus in them. • The animals are weak/tired,they • stop eating and suddenly have a • high fever that comes and goes. Pregnant animals have abortions			
2. Heart water			
• Get it when they are bitten by ticks. • Do not get the disease from direct contact. • Animals become sick 1-4 weeks after they are bitten by infected ticks. • Animals suddenly have a high fever.	• Only works if its started soon enough. • Use tetracyline injections on advice of your vet • Seek assistance	• Spray the goats against ticks	

• They collapse, have convulsions and die in a few hours. • Usually the disease is severe. • High fever. • Off feed. • Becomes nervous and easily excited. • They are uncoordinated and lift their legs very high when they walk. • Grind their teeth and lick their lips. • They collapse first onto their chest then onto their side.They kick a lot,have convulsions and die after 1-7 days. •			
3.Anaplasmosis			
• Severe anemia • Weight loss • Yellow mucus membranes	• Tetracyline injections on advice of your vet	• Tick control by spraying or dipping 	
4. Babesiosis			
• High fever • Depression • Urine dark red in colour • Abortion • Reduced milk yield	• To be effective the treatment must be urgent • Use diminazine aceturate on advice of your vet	• Vaccination • Control of ticks	
Tick control			

You can control ticks and fleas with Acaricides through	i) Dipping or spraying ii) Topical application on body iii) Tick greases		
Diseases that can cause sudden death			
a.Anthrax			
• Gets it from soil while eating. • Common in places where animals have had the disease before. • Death occurs before the signs can be seen.			
b. Enterotoxcenia / Pulpy kidney			
• Many animals die before they have signs of diseases. • Restlessness,sudden weakness. • Throw their heads backwards and • stretch their legs out. • Some convulsions and die within • 1-2 hours. Affects animals that are well fed or having been.